The Monday Connection

William E. Diehl

Leader's Guide

HarperSanFrancisco
A Division of HarperCollins*Publishers*

Leader's Guide prepared by Dee Koza

THE MONDAY CONNECTION: *Leader's Guide.* Copyright © 1993 by HarperCollins. All rights reserved. Printed in the United States of America. No part of this book other than pages for the section "Materials for Group Distribution" may be used or reproduced in any manner whatsoever without written permission except in the case of brief quotations embodied in critical articles and reviews. Permission is granted to purchasers of this Leader's Guide to reproduce pages from the section "Materials for Group Distribution" for private or group use. For information address HarperCollins Publishers, 10 East 53rd Street, New York, NY 10022.

FIRST EDITION

Library of Congress Cataloging in Publication Data for original title
Diehl William E.
   The Monday connection : on being an authentic Christian in a
weekday world / William E. Diehl. — 1st HarperCollins paperback ed.
   p. cm.
Includes bibliographical references.
ISBN 0–06–061925–2
ISBN 0–06–061860–4 (pbk, acid-free paper)
1. Work—Religious aspects—Christianity.   2. Stewardship, Christian.
3. Christian life—1960–   I. Title.
BT738.5.D564 1993
248.8'8—dc20   92-31436
                                                                        CIP

ISBN 0–06–062857–X (Leader's Guide)

93 94 95 96 97 98 ❖ VICKS 10 9 8 7 6 5 4 3 2 1

Contents

Introduction

"In today's world 'Sunday Christians' are irrelevant. The hymns, sermons, prayers, and creeds of Sunday morning have no impact upon the outside world unless they shape the lives of the Christians during the rest of the week" (p.1). William Diehl, a layperson committed to enabling all Christians to recognize a "call" to ministry in the workplace, presents a spiritual path for living an authentic Christian life in a weekday world.

By introducing readers to a ministry of competency, presence, ethics, change, and values, Diehl helps them discover the spirit of work within and outside church walls. He shares practical methods and inspirational stories to help people become aware of the need for channels of change. In discussing *The Monday Connection*, participants will support one another in their attempts to live out Christian values in the world of work.

Those who embrace the approach presented in *The Monday Connection* can effectively move from living in the chasm between Sunday morning and the workweek to a life of wholeness, competency, and compassion.

Starting an Adult Study Group and Using This Leader's Guide

Harper's series of Leader's Guides provides resources for small adult study groups. Each Guide is based on a widely read book by a well-known and knowledgeable author. The Guides supply suggestions for forming small groups and for leading the discussion, and include discussion questions and other material that can be photocopied for participants.

Although designed for use in Christian churches of all denominations, Harper's Leader's Guides may also be used in other settings: neighborhood study groups, camps, retreat centers, colleges and seminaries, or continuing education classes.

Format

Harper's Leader's Guides have been planned as the basis for six weeks of one-hour sessions. This amount of time allows for depth and personal sharing, yet is a limited commitment, one that even busy adults find easy to make.

The Leader's Guides can also be adapted for use in other time frames. By combining sessions, you can discuss a book in four meetings. Or, by being very selective with questions, you can plan a single two-hour session. Another option is to use a Guide as the foundation for a weekend retreat: alternate the six hour-long sessions with recreation, rest, meals, and other activities.

Forming a Group

Choose a book that you think will be of interest to people in your congregation or other setting. Inform them of the upcoming opportunity through your parish newsletter and service announcements or by visiting existing groups and encouraging interested people to invite others. It may be helpful to plan a brief orientation meeting for those who want to be involved.

As few as three or four adults joined by a common interest can create an effective discussion group. If more than twelve people respond, they should probably be divided into smaller groups.

Participants should have access to the books at least a week before the first session. Books may be ordered through your local bookstore or from Customer Service, HarperSanFrancisco, 1160 Battery Street, San Francisco, CA 94111, or call toll-free: 800-328-5125. Plan to allow about six weeks for delivery.

When you distribute books, participants should also receive photocopies of "Materials for Group Distribution" found at the back of the Leader's Guide (permission has been granted for leaders to make photocopies of this section). You may want to hand out all the material before the first session, or you may distribute the information one session at a time.

Ask participants to take time to look over the information before coming to a meeting. The prepared discussion questions will serve as a medium for sharing insights, clarifying questions, and reinforcing learning.

Helps for Leaders

1. Be clear in announcing the time and place of the first meeting. If possible, meet in a pleasant, comfortable room where chairs can be set in a circle. This usually encourages more discussion than a formal classroom setting does.

2. Choose a leadership style: one person may direct the discussion in all six sessions, or there may be two people who work together every session or alternate sessions. Leadership may also be rotated among the participants.

3. "Materials for Group Distribution," found at the back of the Guide, can be photocopied for your group.

4. The Leader's Guide contains several kinds of questions. Some focus on what the book says. Do not neglect these, as they are

basic to intelligent discussion. There are also good questions for drawing more reluctant members into the conversation. Others deal with the meaning and implications of the author's words. And some ask participants to share their experiences, ideas, and feelings.

5. In the Leader's Guide you will find sample responses to the questions. Do not consider these to be the "right answers." They are only suggested responses, which often direct you to particular passages in the book. Be open to participants' responses that may stray from these suggested answers.

6. Don't feel that you have to complete all the questions and suggested activities in the Leader's Guide. Choose only those that seem most important to your group.

7. Try to avoid having one or two people monopolize the discussion. Encourage quiet participants to share their thoughts.

8. If the group spends too much time on one question, or if it goes off on a tangent, gently move the discussion on to another question.

9. Encourage openness and trust in the group by being willing to share your own thoughts. Try to establish an atmosphere in which all ideas are treated with respect and seriousness.

10. The Leader's Guide contains some suggestions for group process. Experiment with these, and feel free to adapt them to your particular group.

Preparing for Session 1

If you have not already done so, read through *The Monday Connection* so you will have an overview of the whole book. Also read the entire Leader's Guide.

The keys to understanding William Diehl's perception of the spirituality of work lie in the five ministries:

- *The ministry of competency:* serving the world by making it a more dependable place in which to live.

- *The ministry of presence:* becoming the channel through which God's presence is manifested in interpersonal relationships.

- *The ministry of ethics:* finding ways to translate biblical teachings into ethical decision making for our complex society.

- *The ministry of change:* working for justice within the structures of society.

- *The ministry of values:* taking an honest look at our life-styles.

At least a week before the first session, arrange to give each participant a copy of *The Monday Connection* and a photocopy of the discussion guide for session 1, located at the back of this Leader's Guide. (You may wish to hand out all the "Materials for Group Distribution" at this time.) Ask participants to read the Introduction and chapter 1 of *The Monday Connection* and answer the discussion questions for session 1 before the group meets.

If possible, do this in a brief meeting. If this is not practical, inform participants as to when and where they can pick up their materials. Be sure the time and place of meeting is clear. Remind participants that they will need to bring writing paper and a pen or pencil to all sessions. Group members may find it useful to keep a notebook in which they can record answers to discussion questions and take notes for each session.

Once you have read the book, review the Introduction and chapter 1 of *The Monday Connection* and work through the questions for session 1. By answering the questions before consulting the suggested responses in the Leader's Guide, you will be better prepared to lead the group.

Check the "Session Materials" list for session 1 and gather all needed supplies.

Plan to arrive early enough for the first session to arrange the room in a way that encourages free conversation. Say a brief prayer for God to be with you and all the participants in the group, and prepare to enjoy yourself!

Session 1: The Sunday/Monday Gap

The Monday Connection, Introduction and part 1

Session Objectives

- To become acquainted with participants and with the theme of *The Monday Connection*

- To consider factors of ministry regarding the mission of the church

- To explore factors that lead to the Sunday/Monday gap

Session Materials

- Copies of *The Monday Connection* for newcomers

- Extra photocopies of the discussion guide for session 1

- 3" x 5" cards

- A Bible for each participant

- Chalkboard and chalk; or large poster paper and markers; or overhead projector and blank transparencies

- Masking tape

- Photocopies of the discussion guide for session 2 for distribution to each member

Opening

As participants enter, hand out 3" x 5" cards and pens or pencils. Ask members to write down their name, address, educational background, and a brief description of their immediate family. When all have finished, have them turn their cards over and, using none of the information just listed, write their vocation (inside or outside the home) and four or five descriptive phrases about themselves. Next, ask everyone to pair off with someone and share the descriptive phrases. After a few minutes, regather the group and take turns introducing each other (make sure someone introduces you as well).

If most participants already know one another, have each make a list of all the kinds of work (paid or unpaid) he or she has done and then choose which work was most or least satisfying. Break into pairs to share this work ministry.

After you regather as a group, call attention to this quote from *The Monday Connection:*

> [1] The mission of the church is to transform lives; [2] its failure to do so in recent years can be measured by its own body count. [3] The rhetoric of the church is a call for all its members to serve God in their daily lives; [4] the reality is that there is a huge wall separating people's Sunday experience from their Monday experience. (p. 2)

Giving participants time to reflect on the statement, ask them to choose one of the four parts of it that they would like to explore in more detail. Let each person read aloud the phrase he or she has chosen. After everyone has shared, divide the group into phrase groups (gathering all those who chose the same phrases).

Allow members to share with one another why they chose their phrase. A recorder may list the reasons and the relationship between the phrase and their vocational and church lives.

Regather into a single group, and ask each recorder to report the insights and reflections discussed. (One to two minutes for each recorder ought to be sufficient.)

Reflecting Together

Begin the discussion of *The Monday Connection*, chapter 1, using the questions from the discussion guide. Allow ten minutes at the end of the session for "Looking Ahead" and "Closing."

1. **William Diehl writes, "My Sunday experience had no connection to my Monday world" (p. 10). On the line below, mark your experience or agreement with his statement.**

Strongly disagree   Strongly agree

Read aloud the last paragraph on page 10 of *The Monday Connection*. Ask participants to share their level of agreement. Comments will vary. Remind the group that there are no right or wrong interpretations.

2. **On Sunday mornings, we are admonished to let our light shine so that others will know who we are as Christians (Matt. 5:16). What does that mean to you, and how are you already doing this?**

Ask someone to read Matthew 5:13–16 aloud as a background for beginning discussion.

3. **Do you feel that there is a gap between the rhetoric of the church and the reality of the workplace? If so, does this present a difficulty in being a disciple of Christ? Why or why not?**

Before beginning to wrestle with this question, read aloud the third paragraph on page 12, beginning "The gap between the rhetoric. . . ." Divide the group in half, and direct one group to look at what Diehl sees as the rhetoric of the church. Have the other look into some of the realities of the workplace that present difficulties for Christians. Request that each half record thoughts on a large sheet of newsprint or the chalkboard and be prepared to summarize and discuss their ideas when everyone regathers. Help the class explore rather than debate one another's findings.

4. **The Bible tells us that at baptism we are all called by God into a universal priesthood. How do you bridge the gap between the priesthood of the church and the realities of the workplace?**

Allow for a variety of perspectives on this question. Review Diehl's statement on page 12. You may want to have members recall experiences where they witnessed hypocrisy between belief and action or bridged the Sunday world (religious beliefs) and the everyday world. Keep note of these on the newsprint or chalkboard.

Read aloud 1 Peter 2:1–10, while participants read along in their Bibles. Ask them what connections can be made between the passage and their discussion.

5. List any ideas or insights from your reading that were especially interesting or helpful to you.

Ask for volunteers to share their responses. Have some ideas of your own prepared to begin the discussion if necessary.

Looking Ahead

If you have not already done so, distribute the photocopied discussion guide for session 2, and make sure everyone has a copy of *The Monday Connection*. Ask participants to read part 2 of *The Monday Connection* and answer the discussion questions in preparation for your next meeting.

Remind members to bring their Bibles with them for future sessions.

Closing

Explain that to close each session, you would like to hold a group prayer. This is done by forming a circle, holding hands, and, beginning with the leader, sharing one meaningful insight discovered during the session. Instruct participants to squeeze the hand of the person to the left when they have finished; those who do not wish to pray aloud may simply squeeze the hand of the person to the left.

Open the prayer with a phrase like: "Dear God, as searchers in the faith we celebrate our discoveries of. . . ." Pray around the circle. You may end with: "For our connections we thank you, O God. Amen."

Session 2: The Ministry of Competency

The Monday Connection, part 2

Session Objectives

- To identify the role of work in the Christian life

- To differentiate between "just doing my job" and "ministry in the workplace"

- To examine the importance of competency in daily ministry

Session Materials

- Copies of *The Monday Connection* for newcomers

- Extra photocopies of the discussion guide for session 2

- A Bible for each participant

- Large newsprint and markers with easel or chalkboard and chalk

- Masking tape

- Photocopies of the discussion guide for session 3 for distribution to each member

Opening

Have class members turn to page 29 of *The Monday Connection*, and request that someone read aloud the Droel and Pierce quote that begins "Until now, laypeople have not had . . ." Ask participants to consider the meaning of that paragraph for themselves.

When everyone has had a chance to reflect (about five minutes), divide the class in half, and ask one group to consider the first two sentences of the paragraph; the other half should reflect on the second two sentences. Allow about ten minutes for people to talk about those elements or ideas in their sentences with which they agree and those with which they disagree or feel most uncomfortable. Instruct each group to note, on a large sheet of newsprint or the chalkboard the important insights they would like to share with everyone else.

After ten minutes, reassemble into a single group and post the lists on the wall. Recorders can summarize their key insights.

Reflecting Together

1. What is most satisfying or meaningful about your work? What is most difficult or troubling?

You may want to break into pairs for this discussion. Follow the general discussion of the question by reading "The Bible and Work" (pp. 27–28). Have the class look for the author's insights regarding being cocreators with God while having to "work hard" in order to exist.

2. In what ways do you experience the tension between competency and compassion in your work? How do you resolve this tension?

Responses will vary. If necessary, review page 46.

3. In what ways does your work benefit other people? How are you acting as a cocreator with God?

Ask for volunteers to share their responses. Draw attention to Diehl's statement on serving God's creation (third full paragraph on p. 39). The class might then consider ways of recognizing and rewarding people in both the work community and Christian community.

4. What are some keys to handling situations like that with Bert (p. 43)—where competition, competence, and compassion seem to be at odds?

Situations like the one with Bert are difficult to talk about, but it is important for the class to struggle with this very real event. Ask participants to consider where competition entered, where competence reigned, and where compassion was demonstrated. Then reflect on an example or two of real situations (if anyone is familiar with one that he or she can share) and how these components were present or absent.

5. What questions or insights about your own work does part 2 of *The Monday Connection* stimulate?

Responses will vary.

Looking Ahead

Ask participants to consider in the upcoming week how they are supported in their ministries in their workplace. Suggest that they keep a list of these ways. Also have them list any support groups that they take part in.

If you have not already done so, distribute the discussion guide for session 3. Ask participants to read part 3 of *The Monday Connection* and answer the discussion questions before your next session.

Closing

Have the class gather in a circle. Read aloud: "Christians are called to be good stewards of the gifts God has given them. We are to be both competent and compassionate. Sometimes those qualities can be in tension with each other. What do we do then?" (p. 46).

Remind the class that Diehl talked about his own struggle in being competent and compassionate but clearly feels that one way to live out this call is to constantly seek God's presence and signs to us in everyday happenings.

Begin a circle prayer; encourage members to pray about areas where they wish for God's presence in being more competent and compassionate. When you feel everyone has had a chance to pray, close the prayer.

Session 3: The Ministry of Presence

The Monday Connection, part 3

Session Objectives

- To connect the Christian theology of grace with our ministry of presence

- To identify characteristics necessary for an effective ministry of presence

Session Materials

- Extra photocopies of the discussion guide for session 3

- A Bible for each participant

- Large newsprint and markers with easel or chalkboard and chalk

- Masking tape

- Photocopies of the discussion guide for session 4 for distribution to each member

Opening

When everyone has arrived, divide the group into triads. Allow a few minutes for the members of each triad to tell a brief story of when they were able to "be there" for someone else. Direct others to listen to each account carefully, and then note the similarities of the actions and attitudes of the people involved. When everyone has shared an experience, ask the triads to choose one descriptive word that characterizes all three examples of being there. Regather into one group and share these descriptions.

Ask volunteers to share how they receive support in their work. What are the connections between their examples of being supported in ministry and the triads' descriptions of "being there"? If any members are involved in support groups, how do they see instances of "being there" lived out in their support group setting?

Reflecting Together

1. What characterizes a ministry of presence? In such a ministry, what type of relationships are we to have in our lives?

Draw the group's attention to the example of Judy's ministry (pp. 59–60). List the components characterized on those pages: not judging, affirming, being present with the wounded, listening actively, and reaching out.

Help the group build a definition of a ministry of presence. Using the characteristics noted here (and others brought up by class), write a job description for a ministry of presence caregiver.

2. What does it mean to be a "priest"—an intermediary between God and people?

Begin wrestling with this question by reading aloud page 61, beginning with "The Universal Priesthood." Follow this by exploring the following passages, reflecting on the meaning and role of the priesthood/priests: Exodus 40:15; Isaiah 61:6a; 1 Peter 2:5–9; Revelation 1:5–6.

3. In what ways does prayer help to keep us in touch with our ministry of presence? How does it influence our role as evangelists?

Many members will have participated and experienced intercessory prayers, but they may not know the formal name of this type of prayer. It might helpful to call attention to the explanation of intercessory prayer given in the first full paragraph on page 64.

Keeping the meaning of intercessory prayer in mind, have someone read Diehl's account of Bob's prayer (pp. 62–64, beginning at "Intercessory Prayer"). Ask the group to identify the components of intercessory prayer used in the "experiment," the link to evangelism that grew out of the event, and the power of intercessory prayer.

4. We are all in need of God's grace. What does the story of Claire and Michael (pp. 73–75) have to do with grace? How does risk taking enter into this story?

Divide the class in half (or into smaller units), and assign each group either the roles of Claire and Michael or of Judy and Bill Diehl. Direct the groups to review the caregiving experience and note those events of grace and those in need of grace. Give participants five to ten minutes for discussion and regather the group. Examine the small groups' findings, beginning with Claire and Michael and then covering Judy and Bill Diehl.

End the discussion of Claire and Michael by addressing the issue of risk taking.

5. Living in a competitive society elevates the "theology" of works so that our identities are largely established by what we do and our worth by how well we do it. How does this affect our understanding of the theology of grace, which says that in the eyes of God, no one is of greater value than another?

To address this potentially volatile question, begin by checking the level of agreement in the class to this statement: "Clearly, then, our identity is largely established by what we do and our worth by how well we do it. We keep score by accumulating wealth, power, and prestige" (page 79).

Ask participants to bring up situations in the workplace where the theology of grace is practiced. Then, conversely, ask for examples of the theology of works. Spend a few minutes discussing and comparing these examples. Which feels more appropriate to individuals?

Looking Ahead

Have the participants try their own intercessory prayer experiment during the upcoming week. Ask each to choose someone in his or her workplace and take the time to pray on behalf of that person. Suggest that recording the prayers or any feelings about the experiment in a journal might make the experiment more meaningful.

If you have not already done so, distribute the discussion guide for session 4. Ask everyone to read part 4 of *The Monday Connection*.

Closing

As everyone gathers in a circle for the closing prayer, solicit names of people to be remembered in prayer (this may certainly include participants themselves). Make a list of the people and include them in the opening of the intercessory prayer. Ask God to be present with them and with all of the group members as they strive to be channels of God's grace in the upcoming week. Allow members to pray as they wish, going around the circle, and close the prayer.

Session 4: The Ministry of Ethics

The Monday Connection, part 4

Session Objectives

- To identify five current misconceptions about ethics

- To consider ways in which the church can take an active role in correcting these misconceptions

- To determine ways to live the biblical ethics of freedom, justice, and peace in our larger society

Session Materials

- Extra photocopies of the discussion guide for session 4

- A Bible for each participant

- Newspaper and magazine articles on ethical dilemmas

- Large newsprint and markers with easel or chalkboard with chalk

- Masking tape

Opening

Ask participants to identify ethical dilemmas that they or someone they know have experienced. List these on the newsprint or chalkboard. You will discuss some of these dilemmas in more detail as you reflect together later in the session. You may wish to have copies of a newspaper article that raises an ethical dilemma to use as the basis of that discussion.

Reflecting Together

1. What are some of the fundamental ethical principles of Christianity?

Direct the class to page 87, which lifts up the issues of justice, love, concern for others, and stewardship. Participants may have additional thoughts.

2. In Diehl's opinion, what are the five misconceptions about ethics?

You may want to review pages 88–90. Draw attention to the definition of ethics at the top of page 89. Write your collective definition of ethics on a sheet of newsprint or the chalkboard. Below it, list the misconceptions regarding the definition of ethics, whether ethics can be taught, the idea that good people make good decisions, legislating morality, and the leader's responsibility for the ethics of the group.

3. How could churches help people make better ethical decisions in the workplace?

Churches could provide classes on making Christian decisions, support groups that bring people of same/similar vocations together to wrestle with ethical questions that come up in their work, or a sermon series on Christian decision making. A number of books could be made available in the church library and highlighted for use by congregational members (see "Additional Resources for Leaders" at the end of this Leader's Guide for title ideas). Churches could help in pairing ethics partners—people who agree to check in with one another for discussions of ethics and techniques for making ethical decisions—and arrange for all pairs to meet occasionally for larger discussion forums.

Accept all answers from participants. Perhaps you will be able to implement some of these suggestions through the study group.

4. What is one ethical dilemma you experience in your work? How might the principles of utilitarianism, rights, and justice help clarify your responsibility?

Review chapter 7, "Decisions, Decisions!" and be sure participants understand the terms used in the question. Pair up the group for the discussion. You may wish to discuss in further detail some of the dilemmas identified in the "Opening" section of this session.

5. How might we define the biblical/ethical words *freedom*, *justice*, and *peace* for our larger society?

Draw attention to page 100. If time allows, use a Bible dictionary to explore the biblical meanings of freedom, justice, and peace.

6. How do you respond to the statement that "any economic system must be judged on 'what it does for people, what it does to people and how people participate in it'" (p. 104)?

Do participants agree or disagree with this statement? Discuss what an economic system ought to do for and to people. What suggestions, if any, does the group have about ways that people can participate in the system?

Looking Ahead

If you have not already done so, distribute the discussion guide for session 5, and ask participants to read part 5 of *The Monday Connection*.

Closing

As the class forms a prayer circle, ask one member to read aloud paragraph four and the first five sentences of paragraph five on page 107, beginning at "When the Pharisees again. . . ." Close the session in silent prayer for the love needed to help individuals make ethical decisions.

Session 5: The Ministry of Change

The Monday Connection, part 5

Session Objectives

- To identify the components needed to bring about change in people and in communities

- To experience some of the life changes necessary to be channels for God

Session Materials

- Extra photocopies of the discussion guide for session 5

- A Bible for each participant

- Large newsprint and markers with easel or chalkboard with chalk

- Blank self-adhesive name tags

- Masking tape

- Photocopies of the discussion guide for session 6 for distribution to each member

Opening

As participants gather for this session, give them blank name tags and ask them to write down what they consider one of the most important or difficult changes people may encounter in life (for example, job relocation, career change, death of family member, marriage). Then have each put on his or her name tag and move around the room, gathering with others who have written similar things.

Ask these teams to consider the following: Why do you consider the change you listed important? What are the positive aspects of this change? What are the difficulties surrounding this change? How might God use this experience to bring about change in your life or in others' lives?

Ask someone in each group to record the responses on newsprint or a chalkboard.

Reflecting Together

1. What is it about change that requires courage from us?

Expect a wide variety of responses. Include some of the insights gained in the opening activity conversations. Many participants may relate to the desire to conform to the culture of their institutions. Such desire makes it difficult to step away from the comfortable in order to embrace change. Discuss the level of courage needed to break away from the institutions we have inherited.

When you feel sufficient time has been spent discussing courage, direct participants' attention to the lists created during the opening exercise. In which of the situations does change happen *to* people? In which do they *initiate* change?

Look together at Paul's conversion in Acts 9:1–19, 22:3–16, and 26:4–18. Note the role of change in these biblical passages. Are there similarities here to some of the earlier conversations on change?

2. Beginning on page 114, Diehl talks about triage and change. Think about a social concern in your own life; how might the triage method enable you to be an agent for change?

Be sure the class is clear about the meaning of *triage* (triage is the medical process of prioritizing treatment for patients based on the severity of injury. The term is often used to describe the general process of determining how to utilize talents and resources most effectively). Divide the group into pairs to consider which personal social concern each had wrestled with in preparation for this question. What insights did they glean?

Then coming back into a single group, select one issue the church might become involved with as an agent of change. Consider how this issue does or does not relate to some of the participants' individual issues.

3. Think of one change you would like to see happen in the workplace. Using the force field analysis described on pages 117–18, list what you see as possible steps toward change in the workplace.

Expect a number of differing responses to come from this question. To help the class see the benefits of force field analysis, you might ask a member of the class or church who had expertise in the use of analysis to make a ten minute presentation. Request that he or she do this by using an example of how force field analysis was used in effecting change in the workplace

4. How might the elements for change listed on pages 123–34 help you to bring about the change you chose in question 3?

Participants will most likely list the following elements from the study: self-interest, inducements (encourage them to express concrete examples), and tactics for change (again, ask for examples to keep the discussion going). Be prepared for other responses as well.

Looking Ahead

Request that participants bring to the final session a special gift they have received. Also ask them to bring their checkbook registers and some object or symbol that represents their daily work.

Invite a few volunteers to meet prior to the last session and consider Diehl's recommendations for support groups (read "Occupational Support Groups" on pages 51–55 and "The Need for Support Groups" on pages 134–35). They can then help the group consider the possibility of starting a Monday Connection support group, to begin at the conclusion of this study.

If you have not already done so, distribute the discussion guide for session 6. Ask participants to read part 6 in *The Monday Connection* and answer the questions in preparation for your next session.

Closing

Gather in a circle and pray aloud together the Serenity Prayer: "O God, grant us the serenity to accept what cannot be changed, the courage to change what can be changed and the wisdom to know the difference" (p. 113).

Session 6: The Ministry of Values

The Monday Connection, parts 6 and 7

Session Objectives

- To confront our basic giving patterns and explore ways to reorder our priorities in the light of a Christian life-style

- To determine how the church can support and enable the ministry of life-style and make it a viable and important role for Christian living

Session Materials

- Extra discussion guides for session 6

- A Bible for each participant

- Symbols of daily work brought by participants

- Table to display symbols of daily work

- A large piece of butcher paper

- Special gifts brought by participants

- Checkbook registers or credit card statements (for individual use)

- Slips of paper

- Stamped envelopes

- Stamped postcards

Opening

Invite participants to place their symbols of daily work on a table provided in the room. Point out the large sheet of butcher paper on which you have written the words *Worship, Study, Renewal,* and *Inspiration.* Under each word, allow each person to write what he or she needs in order to feel prepared and supported for doing ministry in the workplace.

After all have had an opportunity to respond, gather around the sheet and look at the suggestions under each word. If possible, invite church staff members to join in this exploration, and present the sheet to them at the close of the session.

Next, take some time to examine the special gifts that participants have brought. Ask each person to share his or her gift and explain what makes it special. When all gifts have been observed, ask participants to note some common threads that emerged as people expressed what brought gifts meaning.

Reflecting Together

This session deals with some very personal priorities and ethical patterns of the individuals in your group. Be sensitive to participants' feelings and keep the discussions as nonjudgmental as possible.

1. What does real stewardship include?

Have participants follow along as one member reads aloud the paragraph under "Real Stewardship" (p. 145). Discuss what Diehl means when he says that "everything we have really belongs to God. . . . We are accountable to God for everything" (p. 145).

2. In exploring the ministry of life-style and values, Diehl states: "You can begin to examine your life-style by taking into account your giving patterns" (p. 142). What are your patterns of giving, and how do you determine your priorities for giving?

We can find a quick and accurate record of our spending habits in our checkbook registers and credit card statements. Ask participants to review their entries for the past two months and note where they spend their money. What causes beyond the survival needs of the family do they support?

Members may make notes to themselves regarding how they feel about their giving patterns if they'd like to reflect on these feelings later in their journals. If any are comfortable talking about their spending habits, encourage discussion.

3. In what ways might we as Christians learn to use just enough? What examples from *The Monday Connection* seem desirable and reasonable to you? What other examples can you think of?

After some general group discussion, participants may wish to look back over the insights they gained by reviewing their checkbooks. Pass out slips of paper and ask everyone to write down one commitment to use just enough that he or she is willing to make in the next six months. Distribute blank stamped envelopes. Ask participants to address the envelopes to themselves and seal their commitments inside. Announce that in six months you will mail the envelopes so they can reflect on how they have or have not met their lifestyle commitment.

4. In what ways are laypersons called upon to reclaim leadership in the Christian movement?

Reflect on the vocations of early Christians and the leadership roles they were called upon to exercise. Strengthen this exercise by exploring biblical passages in smaller groups. After a few minutes of study, ask each group to report back regarding the leadership components reflected in their passage. Some likely verses include Luke 5:1–11 (Jesus' first followers), Luke 5:27–31 (the tax collector), Luke 9:1–6 (sending out of the apostles).

5. George Gallup reports that "people are hungering for. . . the means to relate the experiences of life to their faith" (p. 191). Drawing on this study and other experiences, suggest some supportive ways to help make the connection of life experiences to the Christian faith.

Choose three or four concrete suggestions from the discussion to recommend to appropriate church committees or leadership. If possible, follow up on these suggestions at a later date and see if any of the suggestions have been implemented.

6. What are some additional life-style changes you would like to make? What do you need to help you make these changes?

Discuss these issues in pairs. Once each pair has talked about the changes they desire, hand out postcards. Ask the class members to address them to themselves and write one commitment they will make to change. Collect these to mail out *one month* after the course concludes.

Looking Ahead

If you had a committee to explore the possibility of forming a Monday Connection support group, ask for its findings. Invite interested members to form the nucleus of such a group.

If necessary, take some time after the session to set up an organizational meeting time for the Monday Connection support group. Those who are interested can then determine meeting times, responsibilities, and the purpose of the group. See "Organizing a Monday Connection Support Group" at the back of the discussion questions.

Closing

Gather participants around the table containing their symbols of daily work. Take turns explaining the meanings behind each symbol. When everyone has shared, hold up a basin and towel as someone reads Luke 7:38, 44–47 and John 13:5–17. When the reading is completed, either wash the feet (or shoes) of the class members or close by saying: "Jesus Christ, a carpenter and the Son of God, calls us all to ministry. Go out into the world now, being living symbols as servants of all. Amen."

Materials for Group Distribution

Session 1: The Sunday/Monday Gap

Read *The Monday Connection,* Introduction and part 1, "The Sunday/Monday Gap."

1. William Diehl writes, "My Sunday experience had no connection to my Monday world" (p. 10). On the line below, mark your experience or agreement with his statement.

Strongly disagree   Strongly agree

2. On Sunday mornings, we are admonished to let our light shine so that others will know who we are as Christians (Matt. 5:16). What does that mean to you, and how are you already doing this?

3. Do you feel that there is a gap between the rhetoric of the church and the reality of the workplace? If so, does this present a difficulty in being a disciple of Christ? Why or why not?

4. The Bible tells us that at baptism we are all called by God into a universal priesthood. How do you bridge the gap between the priesthood of the church and the realities of the workplace?

5. List any ideas or insights from your reading that were especially interesting or helpful to you.

This discussion guide may be photocopied for local use.

Session 2: The Ministry of Competency

Read *The Monday Connection,* part 2, "Competency."

1. What is most satisfying or meaningful about your work? What is most difficult or troubling?

2. In what ways do you experience the tension between competency and compassion in your work? How do you resolve the tension?

3. In what ways does your work benefit other people? How are you acting as a cocreator with God?

4. What are some keys to handing situations like that with Bert (p. 43)—where competition, competence, and compassion seem to be at odds?

5. What questions or insights about your own work does part 2 of *The Monday Connection* stimulate?

This discussion guide may be photocopied for local use.

Session 3: The Ministry of Presence

Read *The Monday Connection*, part 3, "Presence."

1. What characterizes a ministry of presence? In such a ministry, what type of relationships are we to have in our lives?

2. What does it mean to be a "priest"—an intermediary between God and people?

3. In what ways does prayer help to keep us in touch with our ministry of presence? How does it influence our role as evangelists?

4. We are all in need of God's grace. What does the story of Claire and Michael (pp. 73–75) have to do with grace? How does risk taking enter into this story?

5. Living in a competitive society elevates the "theology" of works so that our identities are largely established by what we do and our worth by how well we do it. How does this affect our understanding of the theology of grace, which says that in the eyes of God, no one is of greater value than another?

This discussion guide may be photocopied for local use.

Session 4: The Ministry of Ethics

Read *The Monday Connection,* part 4, "Ethics."

1. What are some of the fundamental ethical principles of Christianity?

2. In Diehl's opinion, what are the five misconceptions about ethics?

3. How could churches help people make better ethical decisions in the workplace?

4. What is one ethical dilemma you experience in your work? How might the principles of utilitarianism, rights, and justice help clarify your responsibility?

5. How might we define the biblical/ethical words *freedom, justice,* and *peace* for our larger society?

6. How do you respond to the statement that "any economic system must be judged on 'what it does for people, what it does to people and how people participate in it'" (p. 104)?

This discussion guide may be photocopied for local use.

Session 5: The Ministry of Change

Read *The Monday Connection,* part 5, "Change."

1. What is it about change that requires courage from us?

2. Beginning on page 114, Diehl talks about triage and change. Think about a social concern in your own life; how might the triage method enable you to be an agent for change?

3. Think of one change you would like to see happen in the workplace. Using the force field analysis described on pages 117–18, list what you see as possible steps toward change in the workplace.

4. How might the elements for change listed on pages 123–34 help you to bring about the change you chose in question 3?

This discussion guide may be photocopied for local use.

Session 6: The Ministry of Values

Read *The Monday Connection,* part 6, "Life-Style," and part 7, "Making the Connection."

1. What does real stewardship include?

2. In exploring the ministry of life-style and values, Diehl states: "You can begin to examine your life-style by taking into account your giving patterns" (p. 142). What are your patterns of giving, and how do you determine your priorities for giving?

3. In what ways might we as Christians learn to use just enough? What examples from *The Monday Connection* seem desirable and reasonable to you? What other examples can you think of?

4. In what ways are laypersons called upon to reclaim leadership in the Christian movement?

5. George Gallup reports that "people are hungering for. . . the means to relate the experiences of life to their faith" (p. 191). Drawing on this study and other experiences, suggest some supportive ways to help make the connection of life experiences to the Christian faith.

6. What are some additional life-style changes you would like to make? What do you need to help you make these changes?

Note: Remember to bring the following to session 6: a special gift you have been given, your checkbook register or credit card statement, and an object or symbol that represents your daily work.

This discussion guide may be photocopied for local use.

Organizing a Monday Connection Support Group

Secure a team to begin planning for your congregation's occupational support group. Be sure to have church staff representation to serve as a biblical/theological resource.

An Organizational Checklist

1.Select the planners and an organizational meeting date. Choose one person to serve as facilitator.

2. At the organizational meeting, determine the following:

   a. The purpose of the group (for example, to share occupational experiences and concerns, to endeavor to live out faith in daily lives)
   b. The number of participants (6–12 people makes a good-sized gathering; aim for a diverse group of people who work in similar fields)
   c. When to meet (meeting on a regular basis is crucial)
   d. How long each meeting will last (one hour is a very workable time frame)
   e. Where to meet
   f. The type and amount of publicity to let people know of the support group
   g. The overall agenda for the time together, for example:
      1. Open with prayer
      2. A member of the support group relates a real-life situation she or he faces
      3. Other members ask clarifying questions
      4. Everyone explores possible action options (drawing on Sunday worship insights)
      5. Another member is chosen to present a situation for the next meeting
      6. Close in prayer

This discussion guide may be photocopied for local use.

Additional Resources for Leaders

Diehl, William. *In Search of Faithfulness.* Philadelphia: Fortress Press, 1987. Nearly two hundred business executives participated in a study to discern the marks of Christian faithfulness. It presents the sense of call as central to its findings.

Dozier, Verna. *The Authority of the Laity.* Alban Institute, Washington, D.C. 1989. Dozier sets forth a biblical mandate for ministry within daily life.

Dupree, Max. *Leadership Is an Art.* New York: Dell, 1989. Christian leadership in business is explored as "covenant."

Farnham, Susan. *Listening Hearts: Discerning Call in Community.* Harrisburg, PA: Morehouse, 1991. Farnham develops a manual for "discernment groups" whose purpose is to help people sort out vocational decisions by being active listeners and asking the right questions.

Laynet. Available from Dr. Edward White, 5908 Nevada Avenue, Washington, D.C. 20015. *Laynet* is a periodic mailing of current resources in ministry with the laity. Its purpose is to enable congregations to empower their members to fulfill God's will in their daily life and work.

McMakin, Jackie, and Dyer, Sonya. *Working from the Heart: A Guide for Recovering the Soul at Work.* San Francisco: Harper SanFrancisco, 1993. Designed as a manual, this offering presents ways to help people figure out what to do with the rest of their lives.

Palmer, Parker. *The Active Life.* San Francisco: HarperSanFrancisco, 1991. A spirituality for the "uncelibate, unsolitary, and unsilent lives most of us lead," focusing on work, creativity, and caring. See Harper's Leader's Guide series.

Smedes, Lewis. *Choices: Making Right Decisions in a Complex World.* San Francisco: HarperSanFrancisco, 1986. Guidelines are offered for decision making based on a consistent pattern of moral values.

Other Titles in Harper's Leader's Guide Series

The Active Life by Parker J. Palmer

Addiction and Grace by Gerald G. May

Answering God by Eugene H. Peterson

The Coming of the Cosmic Christ by Matthew Fox

A Cry of Absence by Martin E. Marty

Faith Under Fire by Daniel J. Simundson

Finding God at Home by Ernest Boyer, Jr.

Forgive and Forget by Lewis B. Smedes

Freedom of Simplicity by Richard J. Foster

Jesus: A New Vision by Marcus J. Borg

The Kingdom Within by John A. Sanford

Letters to Marc About Jesus by Henri J. M. Nouwen

Life Together by Dietrich Bonhoeffer

Plain and Simple by Sue Bender

The Sacred Journey by Frederick Buechner

Testament of Devotion by Thomas R. Kelly

A Tree Full of Angels by Macrina Wiederkehr

Two-Part Invention by Madeleine L'Engle

When the Heart Waits by Sue Monk Kidd

Wisdom Distilled from the Daily by Joan Chittister

Your Golden Shadow by William A. Miller

You can order any of Harper's Leader's Guide series books through your local bookstore or by writing to Torch Publishing Group, Harper San Francisco, 1160 Battery Street, San Francisco, CA 94111-1213, or call us toll-free: 800-328-5125.